Intensive Practice 2A
Preface

Singapore Math® Intensive Practice is a series of 12 books written to provide challenging supplementary material for Singapore math programs.

The primary objective of this series of books is to help students generate greater interest in mathematics and gain more confidence in solving mathematical problems. To achieve this, special features are incorporated in the series.

SPECIAL FEATURES

Topical Review
Enables students of mixed abilities to be exposed to a good variety of questions which are of varying levels of difficulty so as to help them develop a better understanding of mathematical concepts and their applications.

Mid-Year or End-Of-Year Review
Provides students with a good review that summarizes the topics learned in Singapore math programs.

Take the Challenge!
Deepens students' mathematical concepts and helps develop their mathematical reasoning and higher-order thinking skills as they practice their problem-solving strategies.

More Challenging Problems
Stimulate students' interest through challenging and thought-provoking problems which encourage them to think critically and creatively as they apply their knowledge and experience in solving these problems.

Why this Series?
Students will find this series of books a good complement and supplement to Singapore math programs. The comprehensive coverage certainly makes this series a valuable resource for teachers, parents and tutors.

It is hoped that the special features in this series of books will inspire and spur young people to achieve better mathematical competency and greater mathematics problem-solving skills.

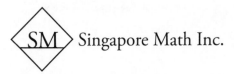 Singapore Math Inc.

Published by
Singapore Math Inc.
19535 SW 129th Ave.
Tualatin, OR 97062
U.S.A.
E-mail: customerservice@singaporemath.com
www.singaporemath.com

First published 2004
Reprinted 2005, 2006, 2007, 2008, 2009, 2010, 2010, 2011,
2012, 2014, 2015, 2016, 2017, 2018, 2019, 2020

Singapore Math® Intensive Practice 2A
ISBN 978-1-932906-02-8

Printed in China

Our special thanks to Jenny Kempe for her assistance in editing
Singapore Math® Intensive Practice.

Intensive Practice 2A
Contents

Topic 1: Numbers to 1000

1. Count and write the correct number in each box.

(a)

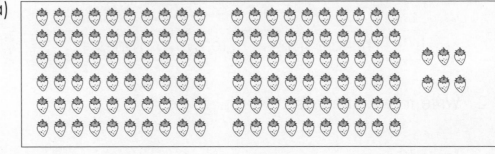

☐ hundred(s) ☐ tens ☐ ones = ☐

(b)

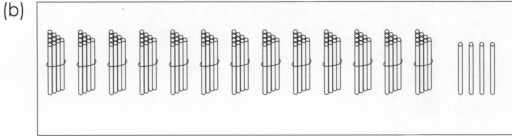

☐ hundred(s) ☐ tens ☐ ones = ☐

(c)

100	100	100		10	10		①	①	①
100	100			10	10		①	①	①
100	100			10			①	①	①

☐ hundred(s) ☐ tens ☐ ones = ☐

(d)

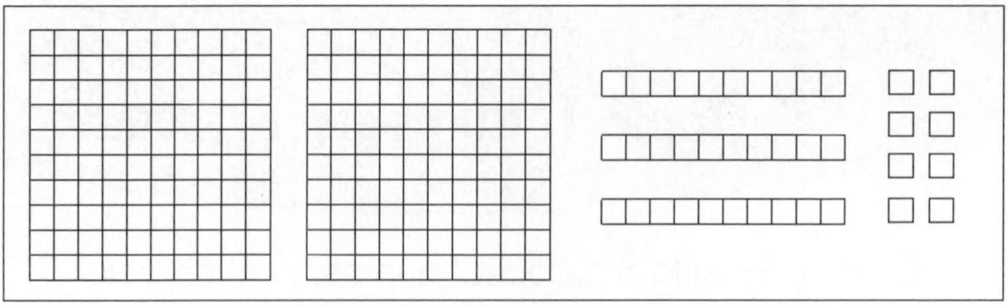

□ hundred(s) □ tens □ ones = □

2. Write these numerals in words.

(a) 712

_____

(b) 308

_____

(c) 945

_____

(d) 621

_____

(e) 850

_____

(f) 1000

_____

(g) 990

_____

(h) 511

_____

2

3. Write in numerals.

   (a) Four hundred eleven

   (b) One hundred thirty-two

   (c) Six hundred nine

   (d) Five hundred sixty

   (e) Seven hundreds, two tens and three ones

   (f) Five hundreds and fifteen ones

   (g) Two hundreds and seven ones

   (h) Nine hundreds and four tens

4. Complete the number bonds.

   (a)
   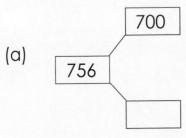

   (b)
   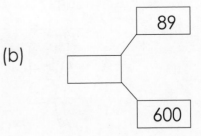

   (c)
   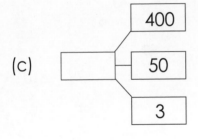

   (d)
   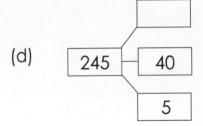

3

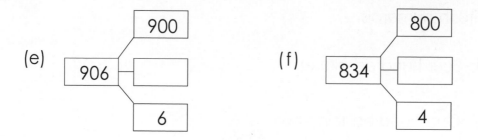

(e) 906 → 900, ⬚, 6

(f) 834 → 800, ⬚, 4

5. Circle the biggest number in each set and cross out the smallest number.

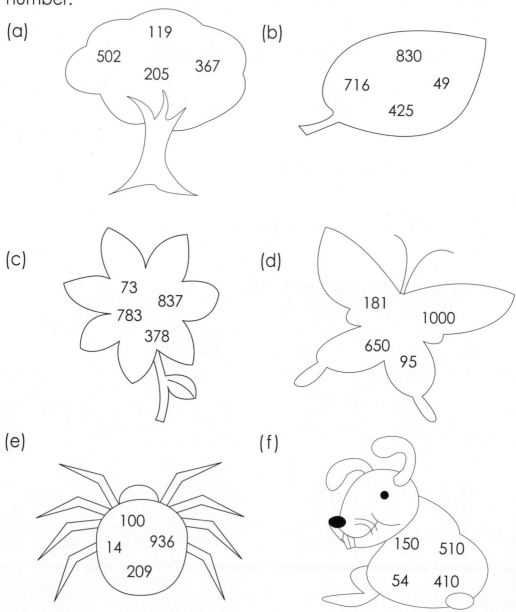

(a) 119, 502, 205, 367

(b) 830, 716, 49, 425

(c) 73, 837, 783, 378

(d) 181, 1000, 650, 95

(e) 100, 14, 936, 209

(f) 150, 510, 54, 410

6. Arrange these numbers in order.
   Begin with the smallest.

   (a) 634,   346,   436,   463,   364

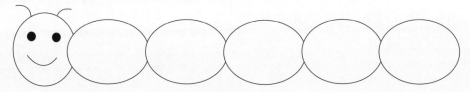

   (b) 9 hundreds, 709, 79 tens, ninety-seven, 907

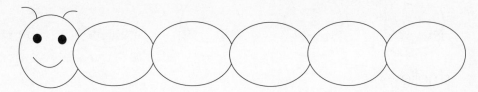

7. Arrange these numbers in order.
   Begin with the largest number.

   (a) 521,   125,   215,   512,   251

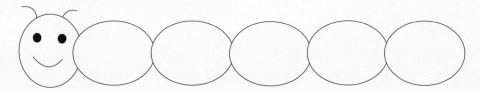

   (b) 8 tens, eighty-one, 811, 18 tens, 108

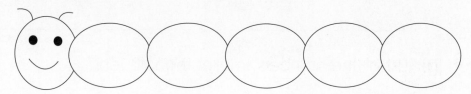

8. Use the numbers in the bag to do the following.

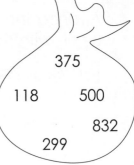

375
118   500
832
299

(a) The smallest number is _____.

(b) The greatest number is _____.

(c) Arrange the numbers in order from smallest to greatest.

smallest

(d) Arrange the numbers in order from greatest to smallest.

greatest

(e) List all the numbers between 300 and 1000.

_____

(f) List all the numbers greater than 30 tens.

_____

(g) List all the numbers smaller than 40 tens.

_____

9. Fill in the correct answers.

   (a) The number after 569 is _____.

   (b) The number before 1000 is _____.

   (c) 823 comes just before _____.

   (d) 141 comes just after _____.

   (e) 760 is between 759 and _____.

   (f) The number between 633 and 635 is _____.

   (g) 1 more than 899 is _____.

   (h) 10 more than 560 is _____.

   (i) 100 less than 426 is _____.

   (j) 115 is 100 more than _____.

   (k) 730 is _____ less than 830.

   (l) 544 is 10 less than _____.

   (m) 371 = _____ + 70 + 1

   (n) 925 = 900 + _____ + 5

   (o) 208 = 200 + _____

10. Study the pattern below.

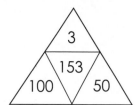 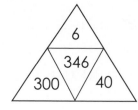 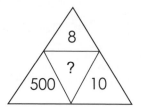

The missing number is _____ .

11. Write the largest and the smallest 3-digit numbers using all the digits given below:

3,   9,   0

(a) The largest number is ☐☐☐ .

(b) The smallest number is ☐☐☐ .

12. Fill in the correct answers.

(a) There are _____ ones in 100.

(b) There are _____ tens in 100.

(c) There are _____ tens in 250.

(d) There are _____ tens in 1000.

(e) There are _____ hundreds in 1000.

(f) 686 = _____ hundreds _____ tens _____ ones

8

(g) 702 = _____ hundreds _____ tens _____ ones

(h) 350 ones = _____

(i) 49 tens = _____

(j) 8 hundreds = _____

13. Name the place value of each digit in the number 204.

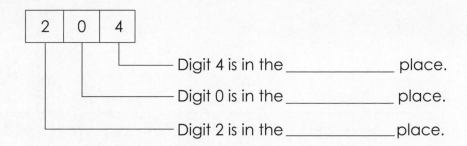

Digit 4 is in the _____ place.
Digit 0 is in the _____ place.
Digit 2 is in the _____ place.

14. In the number 329,

(a) the value of the digit 3 is _____,

(b) the digit _____ is in the tens place,

(c) the digit 9 stands for _____.

15. In the number 846,

(a) the place value of the digit 8 is _____,

(b) the value of the digit 6 is _____,

(c) the digit 4 stands for _____,

(d) the total of the digits 8 and 6 is _____.

16. Study each pattern. Fill in the missing numbers.

(a)

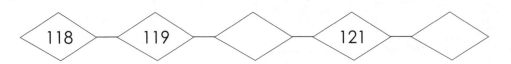

(b)

(c)

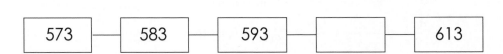

(d)

(e)

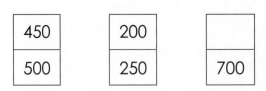

(f)

| 20 + 16 | 17 + 12 | 14 + 8 | _____ + 4 |

(g)

17. Write "more than", "less than" or "equal to" in the boxes below.

(a) 708 is ⬚ 700 + 80.

(b) 35 tens is ⬚ 350.

(c) 100 tens is ⬚ 900 + 10.

(d) 890 ones is ⬚ 8 hundreds 9 tens.

(e) 230 + 4 + 10 is ⬚ two hundred forty.

Take the Challenge!

1. The numbers 1 to 1000 are placed in this order on a number chart.

Column A	Column B	Column C	Column D	Column E
1	2	3	4	5
6	7	8	9	10
11	12	13	14	15
16	17	18	19	20
21	22	23		

Part of the chart is torn. Study the pattern.
Which column does each of these numbers belong to?

423	571	162	850	209

Column:

2. What number am I?
I am more than 20 tens.
I am less than 300.
I am between 200 + 70 and 4 hundreds.
Color the correct balloon.

201   392   268   299   350

3. The squares in this magic square use the numbers 2 to 10.
    What numbers are needed to make total of the numbers in all the
    horizontal, vertical and diagonal lines 18?
    (Each number can only be used once.)

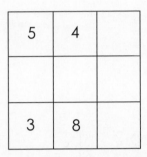

4. What are all the possible 3-digit numbers that can be formed
    using the given digits? (All the digits in each 3-digit number are
    different.)

Topic 2: Addition and Subtraction

Addition Without Renaming

Example: 423 + 135 = ?

We add like this:

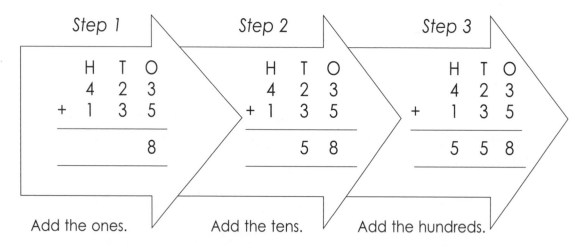

Step 1	Step 2	Step 3

Add the ones.   Add the tens.   Add the hundreds.

1. Add the following.

(a)
```
    3 2 1
+   1 3 7
_____
```

(b)
```
    4 6 5
+   1 2 4
_____
```

(c)
```
      1 9
+   3 6 0
_____
```

(d)
```
    8 5 3
+     2 6
_____
```

(e)
```
    6 0 7
+   1 9 2
_____
```

(f)
```
    5 3 5
+   1 3 3
_____
```

(g)
```
    7 4 2
+   1 4 1
_____
```

(h)
```
    2 6 8
+     3 1
_____
```

(i)
```
    3 1 4
      1 2
+   4 6 3
_____
```

14

Subtraction Without Renaming

Example: 756 − 224 = ?

We subtract like this:

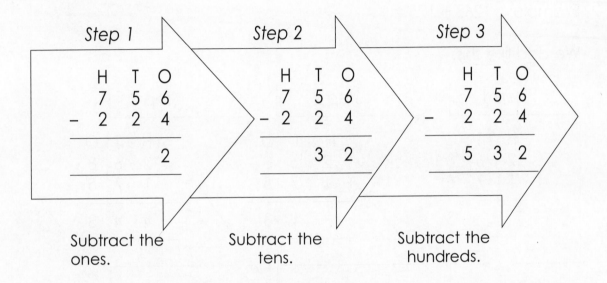

Step 1	Step 2	Step 3

```
   H  T  O          H  T  O          H  T  O
   7  5  6          7  5  6          7  5  6
-  2  2  4       -  2  2  4       -  2  2  4
_____      _____      _____
         2             3  2          5  3  2
```

Subtract the ones.   Subtract the tens.   Subtract the hundreds.

2.   Subtract the following.

(a)   6 7 9   (b)   2 5 8   (c)   4 1 9
      − 1 3 2   −   1 7   − 1 0 6

(d)   3 8 6   (e)   9 6 7   (f)   8 9 3
      −   5 1   − 7 3 4   − 3 4 1

(g)   5 4 1   (h)   1 8 4   (i)   7 1 6
      − 3 0 0   −   8 3   −   4

Addition With Renaming

When there are 10 ones or more, we change 10 ones for 1 ten.

When there are 10 tens or more, we change 10 tens for 1 hundred.

Example: 268 + 175 = ?

We add like this:

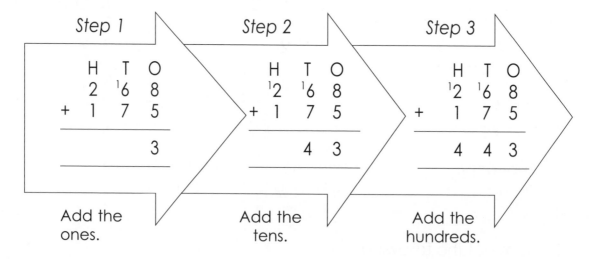

3. Add the following.

(a)   3 7 5
    +   1 3 7

(b)   1 4 9
    +   6 8 5

(c)   8 3 2
    +   6 8

(d)   2 5 6
    +   4 9 8

(e)   6 0 4
    +   3 3 7

(f)   5 5 6
    +   2 5 6

(g)   1 9 7
    +   3 4

(h)   4 8 5
    +   1 0 7

(i)   2 6 3
        2 4
    +   5 4 8

Subtraction With Renaming

When there are not enough ones to subtract from, we change 1 ten for 10 ones.

When there are not enough tens to subtract from, we change 1 hundred for 10 tens.

Example: 523 – 286 = ?

We subtract like this:

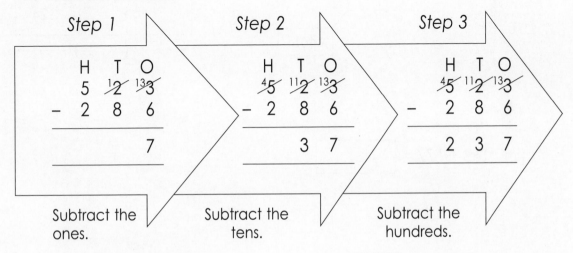

4. Subtract the following.

(a)   5 2 1
      –   1 4 9
    _____

(b)   6 4 0
      –   3 8 5
    _____

(c)   8 1 3
      –   7 6 7
    _____

(d)   4 3 2
      –   9 6
    _____

(e)   3 0 5
      –   1 8 7
    _____

(f)   9 0 0
      –   5 6 8
    _____

(g)   2 1 0
      –   1 0 3
    _____

(h)   7 5 4
      –   2 3 7
    _____

(i)   6 1 6
      –   7 8
    _____

5. Find the values of the following.
   Then complete the number bonds and models.

(a) 324 + 465 = ☐

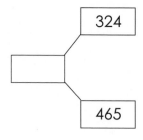

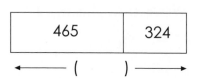

(b) 168 + 577 = ☐

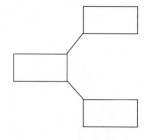

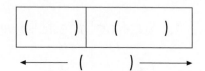

(c) 251 + 19 + 162 = ☐

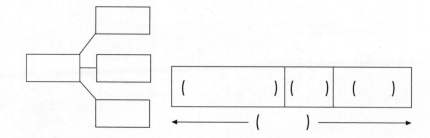

(d) 702 − 238 = [   ]

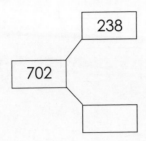

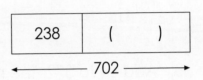

(e) 500 − 79 = [   ]

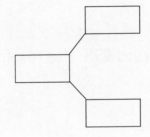

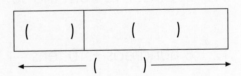

6. Fill in the correct answers.

(a) 295 + [   ] = 430

(b) 726 − [   ] = 158

(c) [   ] − 54 = 211

(d) [   ] + 17 + 325 = 600

19

7. Study the numbers in the jar. Pick the correct numbers to form one addition number sentence and one subtraction number sentence.

(a) [   ] + [   ] = [   ]

(b) [   ] − [   ] = [   ]

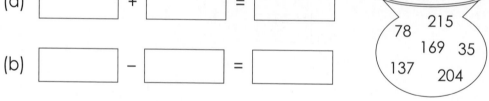

78   215
     169   35
137   204

8. Add 64 to 572. The result is _____.

9. Subtract 149 from 813. The result is _____.

10. Add 386 to the difference between 400 and 265. The result is _____ .

11. Subtract 18 from the sum of 64 and 293. The result is _____ .

12. 8 hundreds + 10 tens = [   ]

13. 2 hundreds + 4 tens + 15 ones = [   ]

14. 17 tens + 633 ones = [   ]

15. 6 hundreds − 5 tens 9 ones = [   ]

16. _____ is 37 less than 502.

17. 645 is _____ more than 385 − 41.

18. 422 is 60 more than _____.

19. 119 is 45 less than _____.

20. _____ is 186 more than 207.

21. 3 tens 5 ones = 2 tens [   ] ones

22. 4 tens 16 ones = [   ] tens 6 ones

23. There are _____ tens in 273 + 167.

24. There are _____ hundreds in 465 + 135.

25. 298 + 606 = 400 + [   ]

26. 135 + 144 = 500 − [   ]

27. Arrange these values from the smallest to the largest.

806 + 10	900 − 137	600 + 4 + 115	750 − 15

smallest

28. The missing number to make 438 is [   ].

100 100 10 1 1   + [   ]

100   1 1

29. Look at the table.

Number of stamps	Number of stickers
350	146

(a) How many more stamps than stickers are there?

(b) How many stamps and stickers are there altogether?

30. Fill in the missing numbers.

(a)
```
    2   6   9
+   3  [ ]  4
_____
    6   0   3
```

(b)
```
    4  [ ]  8
+   1   7   5
_____
    6   3   3
```

(c)
```
    7   3   1
-   3   2  [ ]
_____
    4   0   6
```

(d)
```
    3  [ ] [ ]
-   1   2   9
_____
    2   2   7
```

31.

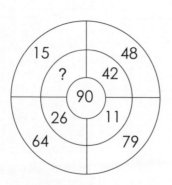

The missing number in the diagram is

_____ .

22

32. Find the number that each fruit represents.

(a) 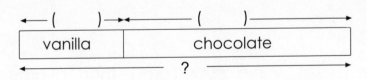 + + = 820

               +   = 600

               = [   ]

(b) 〜 + 🍐 = 80   〜 = [   ]

     〜 + 🍌 = 150   🍐 = [   ]

     🍐 + 🍌 + 〜 = 200   🍌 = [   ]

33. Fill in the missing numbers to complete the pattern.

(a) [   ] , 584, [   ] , 554, 539

(b) 14, 15, 17, [   ] , 24, 29, 35

WORD PROBLEMS

Work out the correct answers. Complete the models.

1. On a hot day, a man sold 57 vanilla ice-cream cones and 176 chocolate ice-cream cones. How many ice-cream cones did he sell altogether?

He sold _____ ice-cream cones altogether.

23

2. For a children's party, Mrs. Lee bought 36 hot dog buns and 24 more hamburger buns than hot dog buns.
   (a) How many hamburger buns did she buy?
   (b) How many buns did she buy in all?

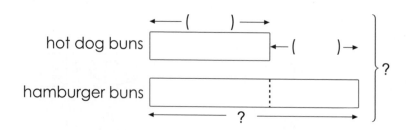

   (a) She bought _____ hamburger buns.

   (b) She bought _____ buns in all.

3. There are 156 first grade students and 205 second grade students in an elementary school. How many more second grade than first grade students are there?

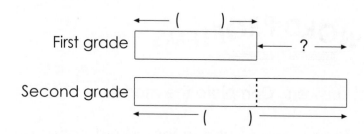

   There are _____ more second grade than first grade students.

4. In a crate of 452 apples, 35 of them were rotten ones. How many good apples were there?

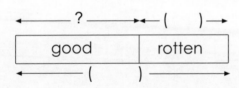

There were _____ good apples.

5. Brian has 33 fewer picture cards than Mark. If Mark has 100 picture cards, how many picture cards does Brian have?

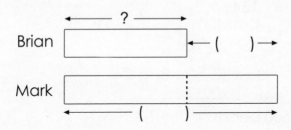

Brian has _____ picture cards.

6. 470 girls went to a music concert. This is 165 more than the number of boys who went to the same concert. How many boys went to the concert?

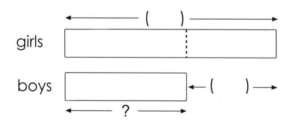

_____ boys went to the concert.

7. Uncle George put 215 red beads into Bag A, 134 yellow beads into Bag B and some green beads into Bag C. He put in a total of 500 beads in the 3 bags. How many green beads did he put in Bag C?

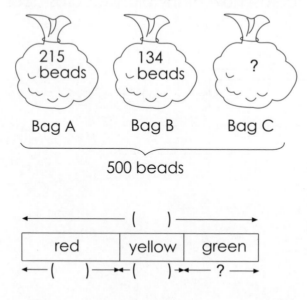

He put _____ green beads in Bag C.

Take the Challenge!

1. Adam, Ben and Charles have some money. Diana has $80. Read the following clues to find out how much money each boy has.

   These are the clues:
   (a) The total amount of money for the 3 boys is $192.
   (b) The total amount of money for Adam and Ben is $127, while that for Diana, Adam and Charles is $202.

   How much money do each of the 3 boys have?

2. Study these numbers:

15   20   35   40   65

The total of two numbers is 80.
One number is 50 less than the other.
From the numbers given above, what are the 2 numbers?

3. Look for a pattern in these 3 strings of beads. Can you find the missing number in the last bead?

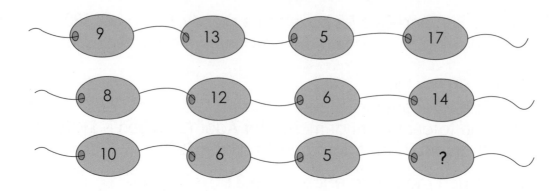

4. David kept some sticks in Box X and some sticks in Box Y. He collected another 10 sticks and put them in Box X. How many sticks must he collect to put in Box Y such that Box Y has 5 more sticks than Box X?

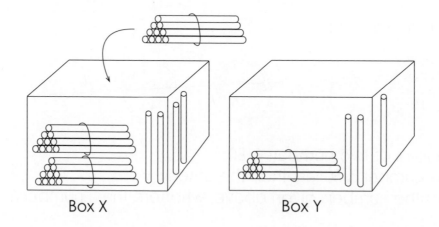

Box X   Box Y

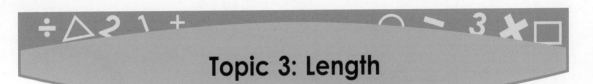

Topic 3: Length

1. Study the pictures carefully. Then write down the correct answers.

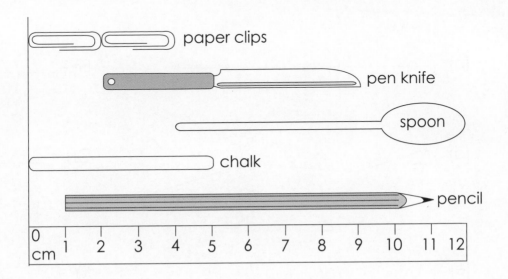

(a) The pencil is about _____ cm long.

(b) The pen knife is _____ cm shorter than the pencil but _____ cm longer than the chalk.

(c) The pencil is twice the length of the _____.

(d) _____ paper clips make up the length of the spoon.

(e) The length of 2 paper clips is _____ cm.

(f) The _____ is as long as 5 paper clips.

(g) The total length of the pencil, spoon and chalk is _____ cm.

2. Measure these lines in centimeters. Write the answers in the blanks.

(a)  AB = _____ cm

A   B

(b) CD = _____ cm

C   D

(c) EF = _____ cm

E   F

(d) 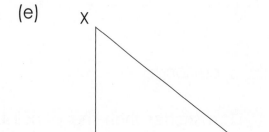 GH = _____ cm

G

H

(e) XY = _____ cm

YZ = _____ cm

XZ = _____ cm

The total length of all the sides of the triangle is _____ cm.

(f) 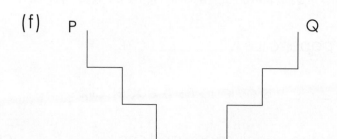 PQ = _____ cm

P   Q

3. Measure these lines in inches. Write the answers in the blanks.

(a)    AB = _____ in.

(b)    CD = _____ in.

(c) 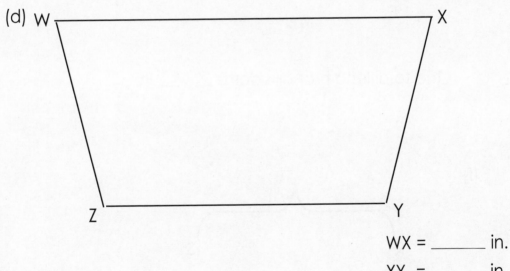   EF = _____ in.

(d)

WX = _____ in.
XY = _____ in.
YZ = _____ in.
ZW = _____ in.

(e)

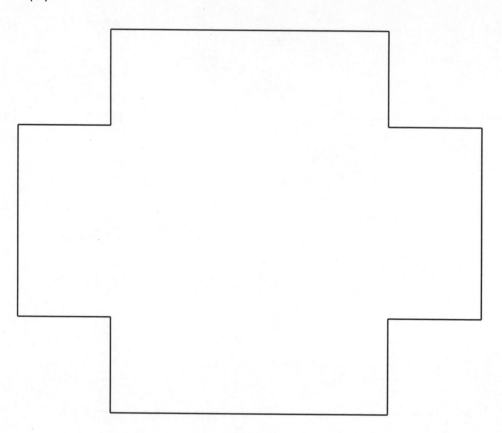

The total length of all sides is _____ in.

(f)

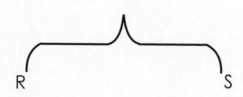

RS = _____ in.

4. Use your ruler to draw these lines.

    (a) A line AB 8 cm long.

    (b) A line 2 cm longer than AB.

    (c) A line 3 cm shorter than AB.

    (d) A square with each side 2 cm. (A square has four equal sides.)

    (e) A line 3 cm shorter than 15 cm.

    (f) A line 5 cm longer than 4 cm.

    (g) A line 7 and a half cm long.

5. Fill in the blanks with "cm" or "m".

   (a) The length of a room is about 5 _____ .

   (b) A dictionary is about 3 _____ thick.

   (c) Mr. Kim is 2 _____ taller than his wife.

   (d) Jeffrey swam 50 _____ of the pool.

   (e) Roy took part in a 100-_____ race.

   (f) The height of a papaya tree is about 3 _____ .

   (g) The length of a paper clip is about 3 _____ .

   (h) A whiteboard is about 4 _____ long.

   (i) Mrs. Fong used 6 _____ of cloth to sew some dresses.

   (j) Joshua is 128 _____ tall.

   (k) A drinking straw is about 25 _____ long.

   (l) Ali cycles for 30 _____ to reach the bus stop.

6. Fill in the blanks with "in." or "ft" or "yd".

   (a) The height of my bedroom is 12 _____ .

   (b) My pen is about 5 _____ long.

   (c) Kyle is 8 _____ taller than his sister.

   (d) The length of a small bicycle is about 1 _____ .

   (e) 2 feet is less than 1 _____ .

   (f) The total length of 2 crayons is about 6 _____ .

(g)   The height of a flagpole is about 6 _____.

(h)   The length of a fork is about half of 1 _____.

(i)   The length of this book is about 10 _____ .

(j)   A computer screen is about 16 _____ long.

(k)   A bath towel is usually less than 2 _____ long.

(l)   Cameron is about 5 _____ tall.

7.

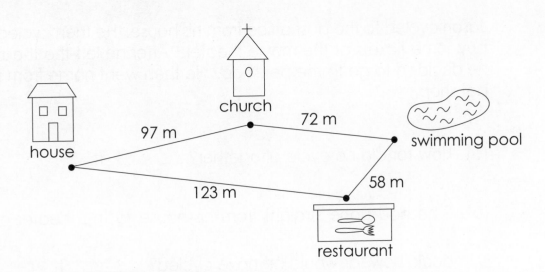

Jessica walked from her house to the church and then to the swimming pool. Her sister walked to the restaurant from the house, and then met Jessica at the swimming pool.

(a)   How far did Jessica walk? _____ m

(b)   How far did her sister walk? _____ m

(c)   Who walked a longer distance? _____

How much longer? _____ m

8.

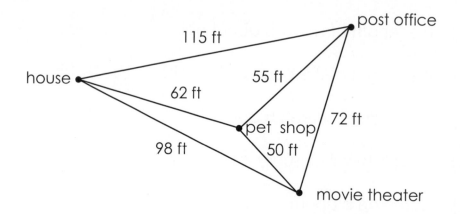

Jason cycled to the post office from his house. He then cycled to buy some tickets at the movie theater. After he left the theater, he decided to go to the pet shop. He then went home from the pet shop.

(a) How far did he cycle altogether? _____ ft

(b) If he had gone straight from his house to the theater and

back, how far would he have cycled? _____ ft

9.

Flagpole A is 3 m taller than Flagpole C. Flagpole B is 2 m shorter than Flagpole A.

The height of Flagpole C is

_____ m.

10.

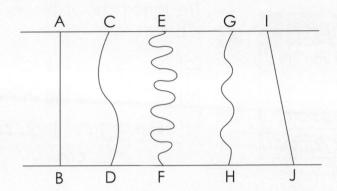

(a) The longest line is Line _____.

(b) The shortest line is Line _____.

11.

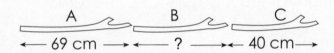

The total length of the 3 sticks is 153 cm.

The length of Stick B is _____ cm.

12.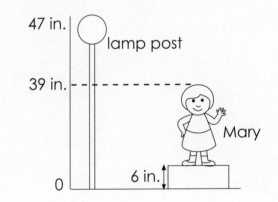

(a) Mary is _____ in. tall.

(b) The lamp post is _____ in. taller than Mary.

13.

Boy	Height
Sam	123 cm
John	140 cm
Rick	135 cm
Kent	129 cm

The chart shows the height of 4 boys.

(a) _____ is the tallest.

(b) _____ is the shortest.

(c) Rick is taller than Kent by _____ cm.

(d) The difference in height between the tallest boy and the shortest boy is _____ cm.

(e) Kent is taller than _____ but shorter than _____ and _____.

(f) The total height of the 4 boys is _____ cm.

14. Which of these lengths is the shortest?
Write the correct answer in each box.

(a) 60 cm,   15 cm,   121 cm,   83 cm

(b) 29 m,   46 m,   11 m,   270 m

(c) 145 cm,   1 m,   20 m,   77 m

(d) 100 cm,   56 cm,   10 m,   214 cm

(e) 88 ft,   108 ft,   99 ft,   89 ft

(f) 30 in.,   3 in.,   33 in.,   303 in.

(g) 13 in., 1 ft, 1 yd, 7 in.

(h) 11 cm, 10 in., 1 ft, 1 m

15. Which of these lengths is the longest? Write the correct answer in each box.

(a) 33 cm, 1 m, 12 cm, 55 cm

(b) 12 m, 108 m, 180 m, 21 m

(c) 124 cm, 412 cm, 124 cm, 412 cm

(d) 8 m, 800 cm, 8 cm, 18 m

(e) 107 in., 71 in., 77 in., 17 in.

(f) 1 yd, 3 ft, 12 in., 2 yd

(g) 100 yd, 100 m, 100 in, 100 ft

(h) 13 cm, 8 in., 1 ft, 11 in.

WORD PROBLEMS

Solve these problems. Show your work clearly.

1. A man jogged round this field once. What distance did he jog?

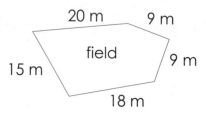

2. A piece of rope 324 in. long is cut into 3 pieces. If 2 pieces, each measuring 85 in. are cut from it, what is the length of the 3rd piece?

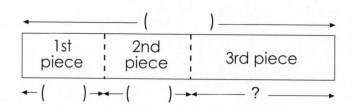

3. Mr. Ho used a piece of wire to make a triangle and a square as shown below. If he had 12 cm of the wire left, how long was the wire at first?

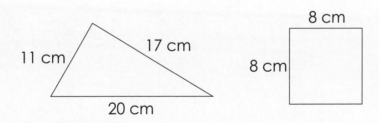

4. A stick is 47 cm shorter than a rope. The length of the rope is 300 cm. What is the total length of the stick and the rope?

5. Leslie is swimming in a 100-meter race. She is 73 m from the starting point. How far is she from the finishing point?

6. Sally is 139 cm tall. Mary is 22 cm shorter than Sally. Betty is 4 cm taller than Mary. How tall is Betty?

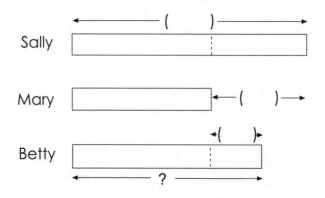

7. Peter lives 305 yd away from his school. Mary goes to the same school, and she lives 298 yd away from the school. Who lives nearer to the school? How much nearer?

8. 2 equal pieces of ribbon were cut from a roll of ribbon. Each piece was 14 ft long and there were 2 ft of ribbon left on the roll. What was the length of the roll of ribbon before it was cut?

9. Kristen is 88 cm tall. Her mother is 58 cm taller than Kristen. What is the total height of Kristen and her mother?

Take the Challenge!

1. A spider is climbing up a wall which is 27 m high. Every day, it climbs up 7 m but slips down 2 m at night. How many days will it take the spider to first reach the top of the wall?

2. Amy, Barbara, Cecilia and Deanna were comparing their heights. They found the following:
   (a) Barbara is not the tallest.
   (b) Cecilia is not the 2nd tallest.
   (c) Both Barbara and Deanna are not the 2nd or 3rd tallest.
   From the above clues, can you tell if Cecilia is the tallest, 2nd tallest, 3rd tallest or the shortest?

3. 5 cars with a length of 4 m each are parked in a row. There is a gap of 3 m between any 2 cars. Find the distance between the front of the first car and the back of the last car.

4. Valerie went to the shop to buy 11 yd of cloth. The shopkeeper made a mistake and cut the cloth 2 yd shorter than what she asked for. Valerie then used 7 yd to make some curtain. What was the length of the cloth left?

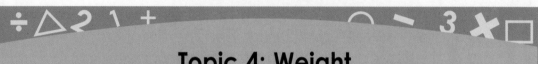
1. Study the scales carefully. Write down the correct weight in each blank.

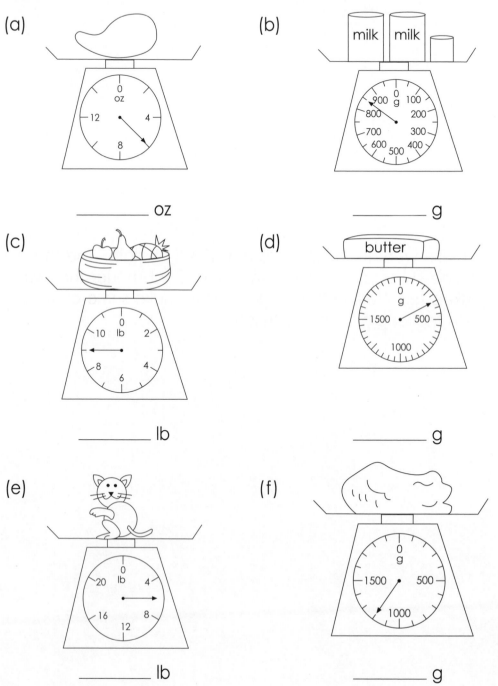

(a) _____ oz

(b) _____ g

(c) _____ lb

(d) _____ g

(e) _____ lb

(f) _____ g

(g)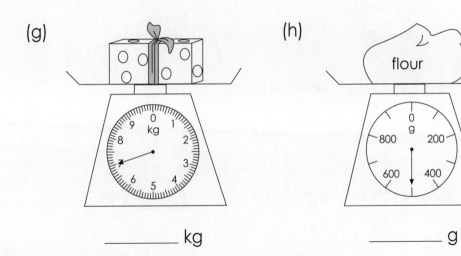

_____ kg

(h)

flour

_____ g

2. Fill in the blanks with "ounces" or "pounds".

(a) An apple weighs about 4 _____ .

(b) A second grader weighs about 50 _____ .

(c) A duck weighs about 70 _____ .

(d) Mrs. Clay bought a 3-_____ bag of sugar.

(e) A sack of potatoes weighs about 5 _____ .

(f) A potato weighs about 3 _____ .

3. Fill in the blanks with "grams" or "kilograms".

(a) The weight of a pen is about 10 _____ .

(b) A cake weighs 1500 _____ .

(c) My father weighs 65 _____ .

(d) Ryan ate 326 _____ of potato chips.

(e) A basket of fruit weighs about 1 _____.

(f) A tomato weighs about 69 _____.

4. Fill in "heavier than", "lighter than" or "as heavy as".

(a) A is _____ 5 kg.

(b) B is _____ 5 kg.

(c) A is _____ B.

5. Study these pictures carefully. Then answer the question.

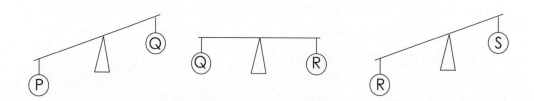

Which is the lightest, P, Q, R or S? _____

6. Each apple weighs the same. Each pear also weighs the same.

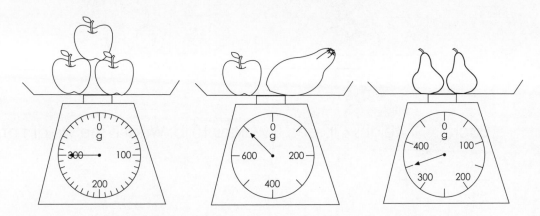

(a) The apple weighs _____ g.

(b) The papaya weighs _____ g.

(c) The papaya is _____ g heavier than the two pears.

(d) The apple is _____ g lighter than the papaya.

(e) The total weight of the 3 apples and the 2 pears is _____ g.

7.

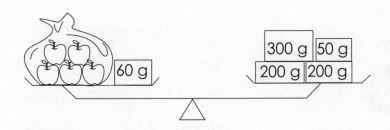

The bag of apples weighs _____ g.

8.

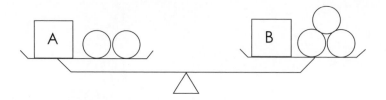

Each ◯ weighs 6 lb and B weighs 10 lb. What is the weight of A?

_____ lb

9.

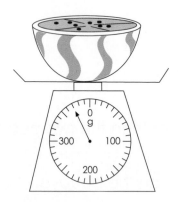

The weight of the watermelon is _____ g. An orange is 155 g lighter than the watermelon. The weight of the orange is _____ g.

10.

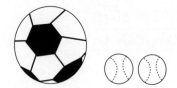

The total weight of 2 tennis balls and a soccer ball is 590 g. If each tennis ball weighs 25 g, what is the weight of the soccer ball?

_____ g

11. 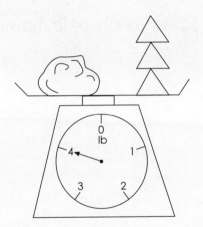 Each △ weighs 1 lb. The rock

weighs _____ lb.

WORD PROBLEMS

Solve these problems. Show your work clearly.

1. A papaya weighs 915 g. It is 530 g heavier than a mango. What is the weight of the mango?

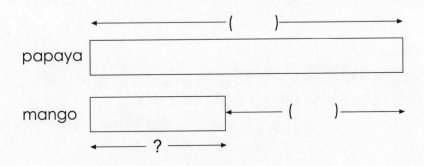

51

2. Sasha is 15 lb lighter than James. If Sasha weighs 84 lb, how much does James weigh?

3. Patsy bought 970 g of flour. She used some flour to bake some cupcakes. If she had 186 g of flour left, how much flour did she use for baking the cupcakes?

4. Box X weighs 240 g. Box Y is 85 g heavier than Box Z. Box Z is 30 g lighter than Box X. Find the weight of Box Y.

5. Study these pictures. Find the weight of the bag of flour.

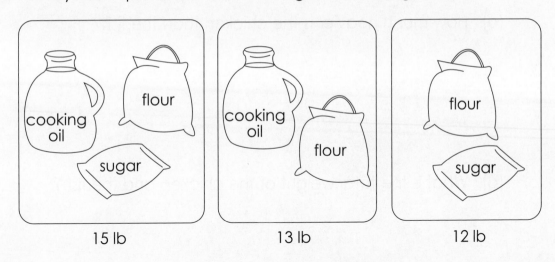

15 lb   13 lb   12 lb

6. What is the total weight of the following items?

7. A chicken weighs 674 g. A fish weighs 252 g.

   (a) How much heavier is the chicken than the fish?

   (b) What is the total weight of the chicken and the fish?

8.

7 oz   9 oz   8 oz

   (a) What is the total weight of these three fruit?

   (b) What is the difference in weight between the heaviest and lightest fruit?

Take the Challenge!

1. From the pictures, can you find out which side is heavier in the last picture — an orange together with a mango, or the 4 apples?

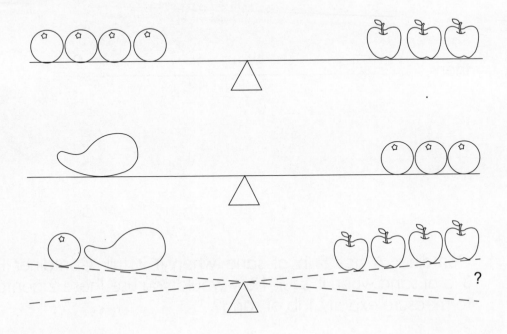

2. There are 4 packages A, B, C and D.

   D is not the heaviest.
   A is not the lightest.
   A is lighter than B.
   D is heavier than A.

   (a) Which package is the heaviest? _____

   (b) Which package is the lightest? _____

3. Find the number of ♡ needed to balance the scale.

If

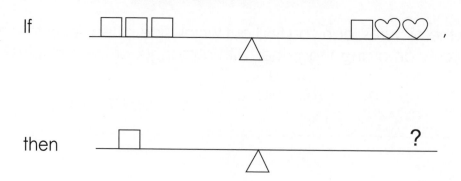

then

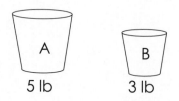

?

4. Container A has 5 lb of sand when it is full. Container B has 3 lb of sand when it is full. How would you use these 2 containers to measure exactly 1 lb of sand?

A
5 lb

B
3 lb

Topic 5: Multiplication and Division

Multiplication

1. Look at the pictures. Fill in the blanks.

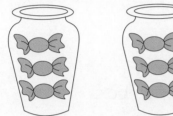

   (a) There are _____ jars.

   (b) There are _____ pieces of candy in each jar.

   (c) There are _____ pieces of candy altogether.

   (d) 4 threes = _____ groups of _____

                = _____ × _____

                = 3 + 3 + 3 + _____ = _____

2. Look at the pictures. Fill in the blanks.

   (a) There are _____ plates.

   (b) There are _____ hamburgers on each plate.

   (c) There are _____ hamburgers altogether.

   (d) 6 twos = _____ groups of _____

                = _____ × _____

                = 2 + 2 + 2 + 2 + 2 + _____ = _____

57

3. Look at the pictures. Fill in the blanks.

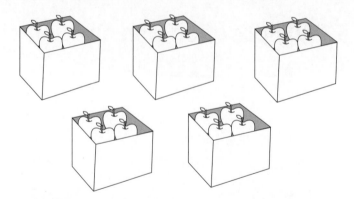

(a) There are _____ boxes.

(b) There are _____ apples in each box.

(c) There are _____ apples altogether.

(d) 5 fours = _____ groups of _____

   = _____ × _____

   = _____ + _____ + _____ + _____ + _____

   = _____

4. Look at the pictures. Fill in the blanks.

(a) There are _____ bags.

(b) There are _____ carrots in each bag.

(c) There are _____ carrots altogether.

(d) 3 eights = _____ groups of _____

   = _____ × _____

   = _____ + _____ + _____

   = _____

5.

2 eights = _____ × _____

= _____

6.

4 tens = _____ × _____

= _____

7.

3 sevens = _____ × _____

= _____

8.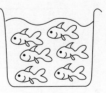

4 sixes = _____ × _____

= _____

9. Draw a picture to show each of the following.

(a) 6 groups of 5

(b) 2 × 10

(c) 4 threes

(d) 3 nines

10. Write 2 multiplication sentences for each set of pictures.

(a)

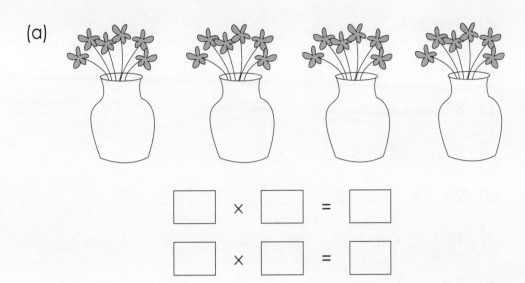

⬜ × ⬜ = ⬜

⬜ × ⬜ = ⬜

(b)

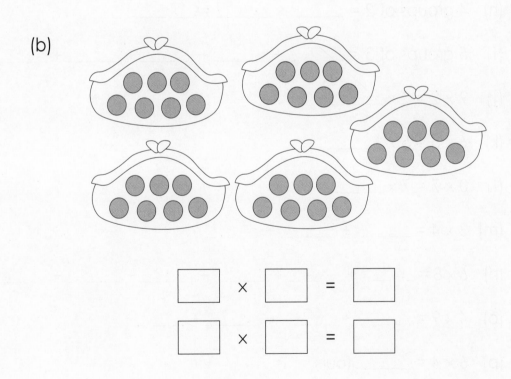

⬜ × ⬜ = ⬜

⬜ × ⬜ = ⬜

11. Fill in the blanks.

(a) 5 nines = _____ × _____ = _____

(b) 6 threes = _____ × _____ = _____

(c) 8 fives = _____ × _____ = _____

(d) 10 groups of 3 = _____ × _____ = _____

(e) 2 + 2 + 2 + 2 + 2 = _____ × _____ = _____

(f) 10 + 10 + 10 + 10 + 10 + 10 = _____ × _____ = _____

(g) 3 + 3 + 3 + 3 = _____ × _____ = _____

(h) 4 groups of 2 = _____ × _____ = _____

(i) 5 groups of 3 = _____ + _____ + _____ + _____ + _____

(j) 9 × 2 = 2 × _____

(k) 6 × 5 = 5 × _____

(l) 0 × 7 = 7 × _____

(m) 3 × 4 = _____ + _____ + _____

(n) 6 × 8 = _____ + _____ + _____ + _____ + _____ + _____

(o) 4 × 9 = _____ + _____ + _____ + _____

(p) 6 × 4 = _____ fours

(q) 7 × 2 = _____ twos

(r) 5 × 10 = _____ tens

Division

12. Divide 14 beans into 2 equal groups.

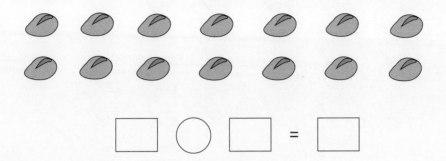

$$\boxed{} \;\bigcirc\; \boxed{} \;=\; \boxed{}$$

There are _____ beans in each group.

13. Divide 12 cupcakes into 4 equal groups.

$$\boxed{} \;\bigcirc\; \boxed{} \;=\; \boxed{}$$

There are _____ cupcakes in each group.

14. Divide 18 cherries into 3 equal groups.

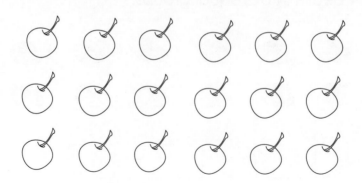

$$\boxed{} \bigcirc \boxed{} = \boxed{}$$

There are _____ cherries in each group.

15. Divide 20 Happy Faces into groups of 5.

$$\boxed{} \bigcirc \boxed{} = \boxed{}$$

There are _____ groups.

There are _____ Happy Faces in each group.

16. Divide 30 rings into groups of 10.

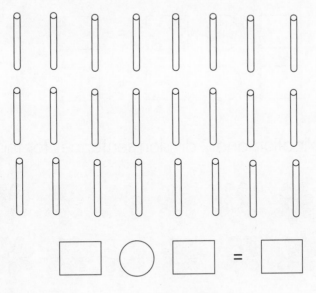

$\boxed{} \bigcirc \boxed{} = \boxed{}$

There are _____ groups.

There are _____ rings in each group.

17. Put 24 sticks into bundles of 8.

$\boxed{} \bigcirc \boxed{} = \boxed{}$

There are _____ bundles.

There are _____ sticks in each bundle.

18. Write 2 division sentences for each set of pictures.

(a)

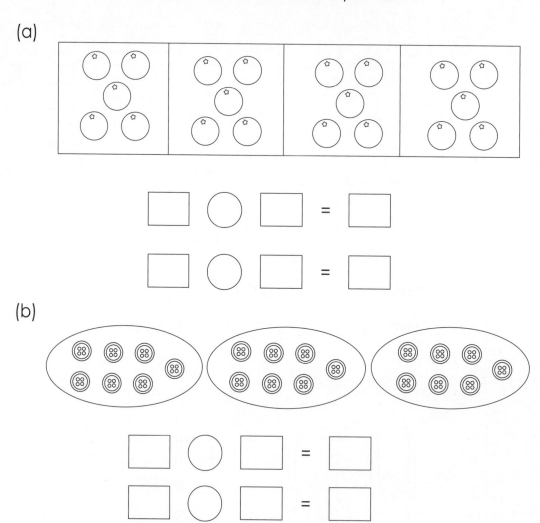

```
[    ]  ◯  [    ]  =  [    ]

[    ]  ◯  [    ]  =  [    ]
```

(b)

```
[    ]  ◯  [    ]  =  [    ]

[    ]  ◯  [    ]  =  [    ]
```

19. Write 2 multiplication and 2 division sentences for this picture.

☐ ◯ ☐ = ☐   ☐ ◯ ☐ = ☐

☐ ◯ ☐ = ☐   ☐ ◯ ☐ = ☐

20. Fill in the blanks.

(a) $3 \times 4 = 12$

$4 \times 3 = $ _____

$12 \div 4 = $ _____

$12 \div 3 = $ _____

(b) $8 \times 2 = 16$

$2 \times 8 = $ _____

$16 \div 2 = $ _____

$16 \div 8 = $ _____

(c) $6 \times 5 = 30$

_____ $\times 6 = 30$

$30 \div $ _____ $= 6$

$30 \div $ _____ $= 5$

(d) $9 \times 4 = 36$

_____ $\times 9 = 36$

$36 \div 9 = $ _____

_____ $\div 4 = 9$

(e)

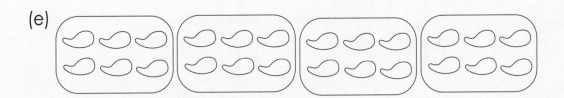

$24 \div 6 = $ _____

(f)

☆☆ ☆☆ ☆☆ ☆☆ ☆☆

$10 \div 5 = $ _____

21. Circle these division facts in 2 different ways.

(a) $12 \div 2 = 6$

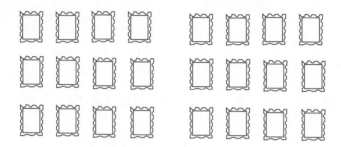

(b) $21 \div 3 = 7$

(c) $15 \div 5 = 3$

(d) 40 ÷ 10 = 4

WORD PROBLEMS

Solve these problems. Show your work clearly.

1. Bob, Alex and Tom shared 21 crayons equally. How many crayons did each boy get?

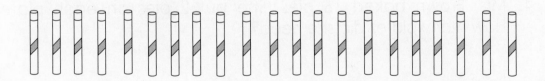

Each boy got _____ crayons.

2. There are 10 muffins in each box. How many muffins are there in 2 boxes?

 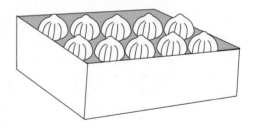

Thre are _____ muffins in 2 boxes.

3. One T-shirt costs $9. How much do 3 such T-shirts cost?

3 such T-shirts cost _____

4. Mrs. Brown baked 16 pies. She put 2 pies on each plate. How many plates did she need?

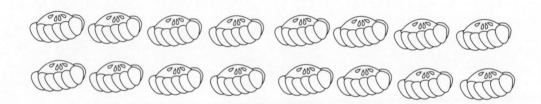

She needed _____ plates.

5. I drink 2 glasses of milk every day. How many glasses of milk will I drink from Monday to Thursday?

I will drink _____ glasses of milk from Monday to Thursday.

6. 5 children made 20 paper boats altogether. Each child made the same number of paper boats. How many paper boats did each child make?

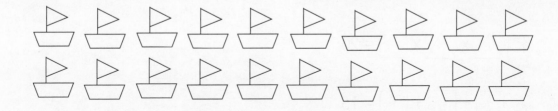

Each child made _____ paper boats.

Take the Challenge!

Fill in the correct answers.

1. $\heartsuit + \heartsuit + \heartsuit + \heartsuit = \heartsuit \times \heartsuit$

   The $\heartsuit$ stands for _____.

2. $\diamondsuit + \diamondsuit + \diamondsuit = 9$

   $\star + \star + \diamondsuit = 13$

   (a) The $\diamondsuit$ stands for _____.

   (b) The $\star$ stands for _____.

3. $\triangle \times \triangle \times \square = 20$

   $\square + \square + \square = 15$

   (a) The $\square$ stands for _____.

   (b) The $\triangle$ stands for _____.

4. Look for a pattern. Find the missing numbers.

5. ▽ x ▽ x ▽ = 8

   □ ÷ ▽ = 10

   (a) The ▽ stands for _____.

   (b) The □ stands for _____.

Topic 6: Multiplication Tables of 2 and 3

1. Count in twos. Fill in the blanks.

(a) 1 duckling has _2_ feet.

(b) 2 ducklings have _2_ + _2_ feet.

   2 ducklings have _____ × _____ feet.

   2 ducklings have _____ feet altogether.

(c) 3 ducklings have _____ + _____ + _____ feet.

   3 ducklings have _____ × _____ feet.

   3 ducklings have _____ feet altogether.

(d) 4 ducklings have _____ + _____ + _____ + _____ feet.

   4 ducklings have _____ × _____ feet.

   4 ducklings have _____ feet altogether.

(e) 5 ducklings have _____ + _____ + _____ + _____ + _____ feet.

   5 ducklings have _____ × _____ feet.

   5 ducklings have _____ feet altogether.

74

(f) 6 ducklings have _____ × _____ = _____ feet altogether.

(g) 7 ducklings have _____ × _____ = _____ feet altogether.

(h) 8 ducklings have _____ × _____ = _____ feet altogether.

(i) 9 ducklings have _____ × _____ = _____ feet altogether.

(j) 10 ducklings have _____ × _____ = _____ feet altogether.

2. Count in threes. Fill in the blanks.

(a) One wheel barrow has _3_ wheels.

(b) 2 wheel barrows have _3_ + _3_ wheels.

2 wheel barrows have _____ × _____ wheels.

2 wheel barrows have _____ wheels altogether.

(c) 3 wheel barrows have _____ + _____ + _____ wheels.

3 wheel barrows have _____ × _____ wheels.

3 wheel barrows have _____ wheels altogether.

(d) 4 wheel barrows have _____ + _____ + _____ + _____ wheels.

4 wheel barrows have _____ × _____ wheels.

4 wheel barrows have _____ wheels altogether.

(e) 5 wheel barrows have _____ + _____ + _____ + _____ + _____ wheels.

5 wheel barrows have _____ × _____ wheels.

5 wheel barrows have _____ wheels altogether.

(f) 6 wheel barrows have _____ × _____ = _____ wheels altogether.

(g) 7 wheel barrows have _____ × _____ = _____ wheels altogether.

(h) 8 wheel barrows have _____ × _____ = _____ wheels altogether.

(i) 9 wheel barrows have _____ × _____ = _____ wheels altogether.

(j) 10 wheel barrows have _____ × _____ = _____ wheels altogether.

3. Find the value of the following.

(a) $3 \times 2 =$ _____

 $2 \times 3 =$ _____

(b) $6 \times 2 =$ _____

 $2 \times 6 =$ _____

(c) $8 \times 2 =$ _____

 $2 \times$ _____ $= 16$

(d) $5 \times 3 =$ _____

 $3 \times 5 =$ _____

(e) $9 \times 3 =$ _____

 $3 \times$ _____ $= 27$

(f) $10 \times 3 =$ _____

 $3 \times$ _____ $= 30$

4. $10 \times 2 = 10 +$ _____ $=$ _____

5. $3 \times$ _____ $= 18 =$ _____ $\times 2$

6. 2 tens 4 ones $= 3 \times$ _____

7. 11×2 is 2 more than _____ $\times 2$.

8. 9×3 is 3 more than _____ $\times 3$.

9. 6×3 is 3 less than _____ $\times 3$.

10. _____ $\times 2$ is 2 less than 8×2.

11. Find the value of the following.

(a) $5 \times 2 =$ _____   (b) $7 \times 2 =$ _____

   $2 \times 5 =$ _____ $2 \times 7 =$ _____

   $10 \div 2 =$ _____ $14 \div 2 =$ _____

   $10 \div 5 =$ _____ $14 \div 7 =$ _____

(c) $8 \times 3 =$ _____   (d) $10 \times 3 =$ _____

   $3 \times 8 =$ _____   _____ $\times 10 = 30$

   $24 \div 3 =$ _____   _____ $\div 3 = 10$

   $24 \div 8 =$ _____ $30 \div 10 =$ _____

12. $24 \div 3 =$ _____ $\times 2 =$ _____

13. $9 \div$ _____ $= 3$

14. _____ $\div 2 = 4$

15. $12 \div 2$ is 2 less than _____ $\times 2$.

16. 3 tens 3 ones $\div 3 =$ _____

17. 2 tens 4 ones $\div 2 =$ _____ ten(s) _____ ones

18. Fill in the correct answers.

(a) There are _____ twos in 20.

(b) There are _____ threes in 21.

(c) If stands for 2 flags,

stands for _____ flags.

(d) If stands for 9 radios, stands for _____ radios, and stands for _____ radios.

(e) One stands for 3 stickers.

Daphne has .

Sophie has twice as many as Daphne.

Sophie has _____ stickers.

19. Circle 2 numbers which do not belong to the set of numbers.

15		12		8
	4		7	
10			20	

20. I grouped 12 flowers in threes.

    I have _____ groups of flowers.

21. Mr. Tan bought a rope 18 m long.

    If he cut it into 2 equal pieces, each piece will be _____ m long.

    If he cut it into 3 equal pieces, each piece will be _____ m long.

22. One triangle has 3 sides.

    7 triangles have _____ sides.

    30 sides make _____ triangles.

23. In the number pattern 22, 20, 18, 16 ...., I am counting in steps of
    _____.

24. Each box contains the same number of cookies. Fill in the missing
    numbers.

Number of boxes	1	2	5		9
Number of cookies		4		12	

25. Fill in the missing numbers.

26. Write a division sentence for this picture.

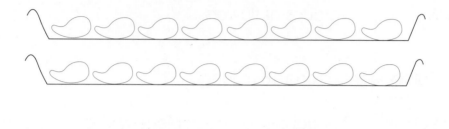

_____ ÷ _____ = _____

27. 2 spiders have 16 legs.

1 spider has _____ legs.

3 spiders have _____ legs.

28. There are 33 apple pies. I put 3 apple pies on 1 plate. I need _____ plates.

29. Peter eats 2 bananas and 1 orange a day. He eats _____ fruits in 5 days.

30. There were 7 boys and 2 girls at a party. Each child was given 2 balloons.

_____ balloons were given away at the party.

31. Vanessa made 8 paper stars.
She made twice as many paper stars as Kim.
Linette made 3 times as many paper stars as Vanessa.

Kim made _____ paper stars.

Linette made _____ paper stars.

32.

Find the missing numbers.

A = _____

B = _____

33. When we add up all the numbers in the ⬡, the answer is the

same as 2 × _____.

34. Which of the following has the largest value? Color it.

2 x 7	12 ÷ 2	2 tens ÷ 2	7 x 3	27 ÷ 3

35. Match correctly.

(a)
  2 x 3

(b)
  6 x 3

(8)

(c)
  16 ÷ 2

(d)
  4 x 2

(6)

(e)
  5 + 5 + 5

(f)
  27 ÷ 3

(9)

(g)
  3 x 3

(h)
  2 groups of 3

(18)

(i)
  2 nines

(j)
  3 x 5

(10)

(k)
  20 ÷ 2

(l)
  2 fives

(15)

WORD PROBLEMS

Solve these problems. Show your work clearly.

1. Polly and Dolly each collected 8 'Hello Kitty' toys. How many toys did they collect in all?

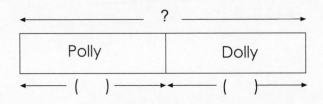

2. Holly saved $3 a day.
   (a) How much did she save in a week?
   (b) How many days did she take to save $24?

3. Five boys and two girls ate all the sandwiches on a plate. Each child ate 2 sandwiches. How many sandwiches were on the plate?

4. Miss Lee bought 6 boxes of tarts. Each box contained 3 tarts. She gave the tarts equally to 2 children. How many tarts did each child get?

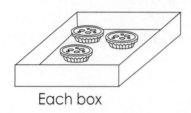

Each box

5. Leslie bought 12 oranges. How much did she spend?

3 for $1

6. Aunt Sally and Uncle George went with their 3 nieces for a boat ride. How much did they pay for the boat ride?

Boat Ride Charges	
Adults :	$ 5
Children :	$ 2

7. Thirty students are divided into equal groups. There are 2 boys and 1 girl in each group. How many groups are there altogether?

8. Maggie sewed some shirts. She used 3 red buttons and 2 blue buttons on each shirt. If she used 18 red buttons altogether, how many blue buttons did she use?

Take the Challenge!

1. Study the numbers in the regions A, B and C.

Which region will each of the given numbers lie?

	Number	Region			Number	Region
(a)	12	_____		(b)	21	_____
(c)	20	_____		(d)	18	_____
(e)	24	_____		(f)	16	_____

2. I think of a number.
   It is between 30 and 99.
   The 2nd digit is 3 times the 1st digit.
   What is the number? Write the digits of the number in the boxes.

3. I am more than 432 – 415.
   I am less than 7 x 3.
   What number am I?
   Circle the correct number.

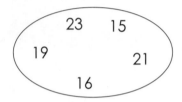

4. You have less than 12 pens.
   You can divide them into 2 groups exactly.
   You can also divide them into 3 groups exactly.
   How many pens do you have?

5. Study the numbers in the first circle. They follow a certain pattern. The arrows are drawn to help you to find out the pattern. Using the same pattern, fill in the missing numbers in the next 2 circles.

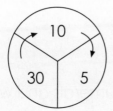 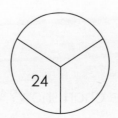 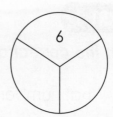

Mid-Year Review

PART 1

Fill in the correct answers.

1. What number does the chart show? Write in numerals and words.

Hundreds	Tens	Ones
100 100 100	10 10 10 10 10	1 1 1 1 1 1 1 1

Numerals: _____

Words: _____

2. In the number 346, the value of the digit 4 is _____.

3. Which has the largest value? Circle it.

16 tens – 48 ones	87 + 245	12 × 3	500 – 317

4. Circle the smallest number in the box below. Add 489 to this smallest number.

302	231
213	320

The answer is _____.

5. 9 hundreds = 500 + 20 + _____ .

6. 47 = 3 tens _____ ones.

7. Form the smallest 3-digit number using the digits 0, 6 and 3.
    The answer is _____.

8. 419 comes between 420 and _____.

9. _____ comes before 1000.

10. 197 is 58 more than _____.

11. 568 is _____ less than 700.

12. There are _____ tens in 950.

13. The digit in the hundreds place in 875 – 386 is _____.

Study this picture and answer Questions 14 to 16.

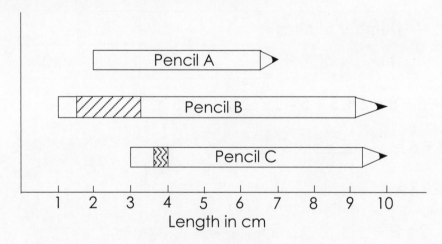

14. Pencil B is _____ cm longer than Pencil A.

15. Pencil _____ is shorter than Pencil _____ but longer than

     Pencil _____.

16. The total length of the 3 pencils is _____ cm.

17. ✏️✏️✏️✏️ stands for 12,

    then ✏️✏️✏️ stands for _____.

18. If 24 + ♡ + ♡ = 46

    then ♡ = _____

19. If ☆ + ☾ = 20

    and ☆ − ☾ = 8,

    then ☆ = _____

    and ☾ = _____

20. Complete the table below.

Number of birds	3		7	
Number of feet		18		10

21. 5 + 5 + 5 + 5 + 5 + 5 = _____ × 5

22. 18 + 6 = _____ × 3

23. 27 ÷ 3 = _____

24. 9 × 2 = 9 + _____

25. $12 \xrightarrow{\times 2} \square \xrightarrow{\div 3} \square$

Complete the number patterns:

26. 180, 152, 124, _____, 68

27. 36, 33, _____, _____, 24

28.

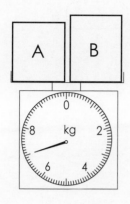 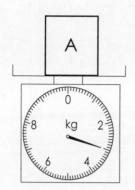 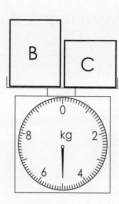

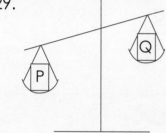 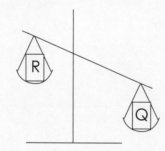 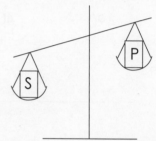

The total weight of Box A and Box C is _____ kg.

29.

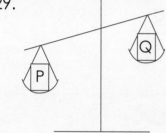

Arrange the 4 boxes P, Q, R and S in order of weight. Begin with the lightest.

_____, _____, _____, _____,
Lightest

Fill in the missing numbers for Questions 30 and 31:

30.
```
    3  1  5
  + 5  □  □
  ─────────
    9  0  0
```

31.
```
    9  □  5
  - 1  8  7
  ─────────
    7  9  8
```

Put "more than", "less than" or "equal to" in the ⬭ .

32. 724 is ⬭ 70 + 24.

33. 886 is ⬭ 907 − 21.

34. 10 tens is ⬭ 1000.

35. Arrange these numbers in order. Begin with the largest number.

 490   409   49   940   904

---

36. The table shows the number of photographs in 5 albums. Which 2 albums contain 392 photographs altogether?

Album	A	B	C	D	E
Number of photographs	308	269	94	281	123

Albums _____ and _____ .

Fill in the missing signs in the boxes.

37. 18 ☐ 2 = 9

38. 24 ☐ 4 = 2 ☐ 10

92

39. Put these oranges into 3 equal bags. Draw the oranges in the bags.

There are _____ oranges in each bag.

40. Pack these pencils into boxes of 4. Circle correctly.

There are _____ boxes.

PART 2

For questions 41 to 50, show your work clearly in the space below each question and write your answers in the spaces provided.

41. Ramon is 47 years old. Manuel is 6 years older than Ramon. How old will Manuel be in 10 years' time?

Answer: _____

42. A farmer had 104 chicks and 65 ducks. He sold 38 chicks and bought another 12 ducks. How many chicks and ducks in all does he have now?

Answer: _____

43. A square made of wire has sides each measuring 3 in. The square is bent to form a triangle of equal sides. What is the length of each side of the triangle?

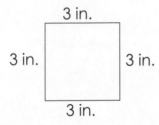
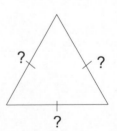

Answer: _____

44. John's father weighs 146 lb. He is 52 lb heavier than John. What is their total weight?

Answer: _____

45.

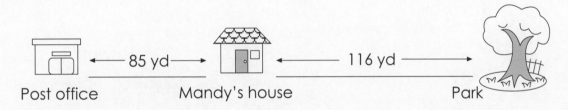

Post office   Mandy's house   Park

Mandy walked to the Post Office from her house and back.
(a) How far did she walk?
(b) Which is farther from her house, the Post Office or the Park? How much farther?

Answer: (a) _____

(b) _____

46. A cup, a bowl and a plate have a total weight of 650 g. The cup and the bowl have a total weight of 500 g. The cup and the plate have a weight of 330 g in total. What is the weight of the cup?

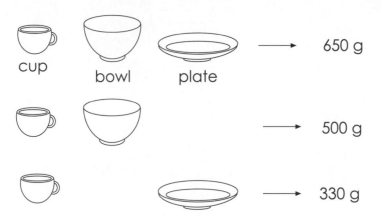

cup   bowl   plate   ⟶   650 g

⟶   500 g

⟶   330 g

Answer: _____

47. Victor puts 5 coins in a row along each edge of a rectangular cardboard. Each corner of the cardboard has a coin. How many coins are there altogether?

Answer: _____

48. Mrs. Knowles bought 50 yd of cloth. She used 18 yd of it to sew some curtains and another 13 yd to sew some pillow cases. How much cloth did she have left?

Answer: _____

49. 30 students are divided into 3 equal groups.
    (a) How many students are there in each group?
    (b) If there is an equal number of boys and girls in each group, how many girls are there in each group?

Answer: (a) _____

(b) _____

50. There are 3 apples and 4 pears in each basket.
    (a) How many fruits are there in 3 such baskets?
    (b) How many more pears than apples are there altogether in the 3 baskets?

Answer: (a) _____

(b) _____

1. Fill in the boxes with the correct numbers so that the three numbers in any horizontal or vertical position make a total of 50.

	9	28					
		18		27			
	10				15		
32						19	
	13				36		
		9		15			
			18				

2. Fill in the boxes with the numbers 1, 2, 3, 4, 5, 6, 7, 8 and 9. Each of these numbers can only be used once to make the total of the three numbers in the horizontal, vertical and diagonal positions the same.

3. In each of the following, find the number of △ needed to balance the scale.

(a) If
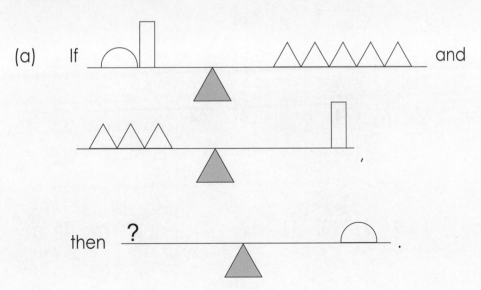
and

then
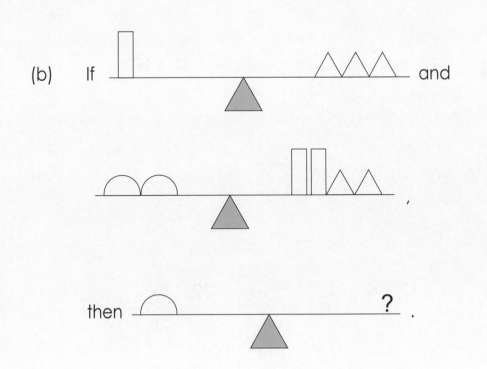

(b) If and

then

4. Fill in the missing number in each sequence.

(a)   97,   93,   [   ] ,   85,   81

(b)   77,   76,   74,   [   ] ,   67,   62

(c)   3,   9,   7,   13,   11,   17,   15,   [   ] ,   19,   25

(d)   1,   2,   3,   6,   7,   14,   15,   30,   [   ] ,   62

(e)   59,   8,   54,   11,   [   ] ,   14,   44,   17

(f)   80,   40,   20,   10,   [   ]

(g)   3,   12,   6,   24,   9,   [   ] ,   12,   48

5. In each of the following, each of the shapes $\heartsuit$, $\triangleright$ and $\cap$ stands for a certain number. What number does each shape stand for?

(a) $\triangleright + \triangleright = 18$ $\heartsuit$ = _____

       $\cap - \heartsuit = 8$ $\triangleright$ = _____

       $\triangleright - \heartsuit = 5$ $\cap$ = _____

       $\cap - \triangleright = 3$

(b) $\triangleright + \heartsuit = 8$ $\heartsuit$ = _____

       $\heartsuit + \cap = 16$ $\triangleright$ = _____

       $\cap + \triangleright = 12$ $\cap$ = _____

       $\triangleright + \triangleright + \triangleright + \triangleright = 8$

(c) $\cap + \heartsuit = 10$ $\heartsuit$ = _____

       $\triangleright - \cap = 10$ $\triangleright$ = _____

       $\triangleright - \heartsuit = 6$ $\cap$ = _____

       $\cap + \cap + \cap = 9$

6. In each of the following, use any three different numbers from the numbers 2, 3, 4, 5 and 6 to fill in the boxes so as to complete the number sentence.

(a) ☐ + ☐ − ☐ = 2

(b) ☐ + ☐ + ☐ = 11

(c) ☐ × ☐ + ☐ = 10

(d) ☐ × ☐ − ☐ = 0

(e) ☐ × ☐ − ☐ = 3

7. The diagram shows a clock-face with numbers 1 to 12.
Can you divide the clock-face into two equal halves such that the sum of the numbers on each half is the same?

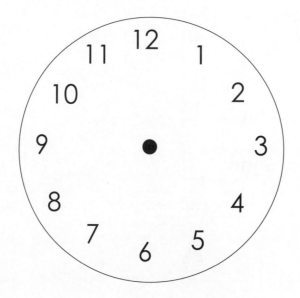

8. If ♡ and ◇ stand for two different numbers, what number does each shape stand for?

$$♡ + ♡ = ◇$$

$$♡ \times ♡ = ◇$$

$$♡ \ = \underline{\hspace{2cm}}, \quad ◇ = \underline{\hspace{2cm}}.$$

9. What is the largest possible answer for the following addition problem if the boxes are to be filled by the numbers 2, 5, 7 and 9 (each number can only be used once)?

```
      □  □
  +   □  □
  _____
        ?
  _____
```

10. What is the largest possible answer for the following subtraction problem where B is not zero?

```
      A  B
  −   B  A
  _____
        ?
  _____
```

103

11. In the following subtraction problem, what number does each shape stand for? Each number is between 5 and 10.

$\heartsuit$ = _____

$\star$ = _____

12. Five numbers 1, 2, 3, 4 and 5 are arranged in a certain order as shown.

1, 3, 5, 4, 2, 1, 3, 5, 4, 2, 1, 3, ...

What is the 48th number in the number pattern?

Answers

Topic 1: Numbers to 1000

1. (a) 1, 2, 6, 126   (b) 1, 3, 4, 134
   (c) 7, 5, 9, 759   (d) 2, 3, 8, 238
2. (a) Seven hundred twelve
   (b) Three hundred eight
   (c) Nine hundred forty-five
   (d) Six hundred twenty-one
   (e) Eight hundred fifty
   (f) One thousand
   (g) Nine hundred ninety
   (h) Five hundred eleven
3. (a) 411 (b) 132 (c) 609 (d) 560
   (e) 723 (f) 515 (g) 207 (h) 940
4. (a) 56 (b) 689 (c) 453 (d) 200
   (e) 0 (f) 30
5. (a) Circle: 502, Cross: 119
   (b) Circle: 830, Cross: 49
   (c) Circle: 837, Cross: 73
   (d) Circle: 1000, Cross: 95
   (e) Circle: 936, Cross: 14
   (f) Circle: 510, Cross: 54
6. (a) 346, 364, 436, 463, 634
   (b) ninety-seven, 709, 79 tens, 9 hundreds, 907
7. (a) 521, 512, 251, 215, 125
   (b) 811, 18 tens, 108, eight-one, 8 tens
8. (a) 118   (b) 832
   (c) 118, 299, 375, 500, 832
   (d) 832, 500, 375, 299, 118
   (e) 375, 500, 832   (f) 375, 500, 832
   (g) 118, 299, 375
9. (a) 570 (b) 999 (c) 824 (d) 140
   (e) 761 (f) 634 (g) 900 (h) 570
   (i) 326 (j) 15 (k) 100 (l) 554
   (m) 300 (n) 20 (o) 8
10. 518
11. (a) 930   (b) 309
12. (a) 100 (b) 10 (c) 25
    (d) 100 (e) 10 (f) 6, 8, 6
    (g) 7, 0, 2 (h) 350 (i) 490
    (j) 800
13. ones, tens, hundreds
14. (a) 300 (b) 2 (c) 9
15. (a) hundreds (b) 6
    (c) 40 (d) 806
16. (a) 120, 122 (b) 700, 697 (c) 603
    (d) 421 (e) 650 (f) 11
    (g) 72
17. (a) less than (b) equal to
    (c) more than (d) equal to
    (e) more than

Take the Challenge!

1. C, A, B, E, D   2. Color 299
3.

5	4	9
10	6	2
3	8	7

4. 157, 175, 517, 571, 715, 751

Topic 2: Addition and Subtraction

1. (a) 458 (b) 589 (c) 379
   (d) 879 (e) 799 (f) 668
   (g) 883 (h) 299 (i) 789
2. (a) 547 (b) 241 (c) 313
   (d) 335 (e) 233 (f) 552
   (g) 241 (h) 101 (i) 712
3. (a) 512 (b) 834 (c) 900
   (d) 754 (e) 941 (f) 812
   (g) 231 (h) 592 (i) 835
4. (a) 372 (b) 255 (c) 46
   (d) 336 (e) 118 (f) 332
   (g) 107 (h) 517 (i) 538
5. (a) 789 (b) 745 (c) 432
   (d) 464 (e) 421
6. (a) 135 (b) 568 (c) 265
   (d) 258
7. (a) 137 + 78 = 215; 35 + 169 = 204;
       169 + 35 = 204; 78 + 137 = 215
   (b) 204 – 35 = 169; 204 – 169 = 35;
       215 – 78 = 137; 215 – 137 = 78
8. 636   9. 664   10. 521
11. 339   12. 900   13. 255
14. 803   15. 541   16. 465
17. 301   18. 362   19. 164
20. 393   21. 15   22. 5
23. 44   24. 6   25. 504
26. 221
27. 600 + 4 + 115, 750 – 15, 900 – 137, 806 + 10
28. 124
29. (a) 204   (b) 496
30. (a) 3   (b) 5
    (c) 5   (d) 56

31. 75
32. (a) 220   (b) 30, 50, 120
33. (a) 599, 569   (b) 20

Word Problems
1. 233
2. (a) 60   (b) 96
3. 49   4. 417
5. 67   6. 305
7. 151

Take the Challenge!
1. Charles' money
   = Total amount for 3 boys – Adam and Ben's total
   = \$192 – \$127
   = \$65
   Adam's money
   = \$202 – Diana's money – Charles' money
   = \$202 – \$80 – \$65
   = \$57
   Ben's money = \$127 – Adam's money
                 = \$127 – 57
                 = \$70
2. 65 + 15 = 80; 65 – 15 = 50.
   The 2 numbers are 65 and 15.
3. The signs + and – alternate:
   9 + 13 = 22, 22 – 5 = 17;
   8 + 12 = 20, 20 – 6 = 14;
   10 + 6 = 16, 16 – 5 = 11.
   The answer is 11.
   Alternative:

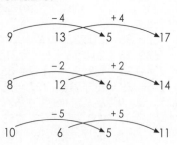

4. Total no. of sticks in Box X = 24 + 10 = 34;
   34 + 5 = 39
   The answer is 39 – 13 = 26.

Topic 3: Length
1. (a) 10   (b) 3, 2   (c) chalk
   (d) 4   (e) 4   (f) pencil
   (g) 23

2. (a) 5   (b) 9   (c) 7
   (d) 8   (e) 12   (f) 12
3. (a) 2   (b) 3   (c) 4
   (d) WX = 4, XY = 2, YZ = 3, ZW = 2
   (e) 18   (f) 3
5. (a) m   (b) cm   (c) cm
   (d) m   (e) m   (f) m
   (g) cm   (h) m   (i) m
   (j) cm   (k) cm   (l) m
6. (a) ft   (b) in.   (c) in.
   (d) yd   (e) yd   (f) in.
   (g) yd   (h) ft   (i) in.
   (j) in.   (k) yd   (l) ft
7. (a) 169   (b) 181
   (c) Jessica's sister, 12
8. (a) 299   (b) 196
9. 4
10. (a) EF   (b) AB
11. 44
12. (a) 33   (b) 14
13. (a) John   (b) Sam
   (c) 6   (d) 17
   (e) Sam, Rick, John   (f) 527
14. (a) 15 cm   (b) 11 m
   (c) 1 m   (d) 56 cm
   (e) 88 ft   (f) 3 in.
   (g) 7 in.   (h) 11 cm
15. (a) 1 m   (b) 180 m
   (c) 142 m   (d) 18 m
   (e) 107 in.   (f) 2 yd
   (g) 100 m   (h) 1 ft

Word Problems
1. 71 m   2. 154 in.
3. 92 cm   4. 553 cm
5. 27 m   6. 121 cm
7. Mary, 7 yd   8. 30 ft
9. 234 cm

Take the Challenge!
1. In 1 day, it climbs 7 – 2 = 5 m
   In 4 days, it climbs 5 + 5 + 5 + 5 = 20 m
   On the 5th day, it will climb 20 + 7 = 27 m.
   It will take 5 days.
2. 3rd tallest
3. 4 + 4 + 4 + 4 + 4 = 20 m
   3 + 3 + 3 + 3 = 12 m
   Distance = 20 + 12 = 32 m
4. 2 yd

Topic 4: Weight

1. (a) 6 oz   (b) 850 g
   (c) 9 lb   (d) 350 g
   (e) 6 lb   (f) 1200 g
   (g) 7 kg   (h) 500 g
2. (a) ounces   (b) pounds
   (c) ounces   (d) pounds
   (e) pounds   (f) ounces
3. (a) grams   (b) grams
   (c) kilograms   (d) grams
   (e) kilograms   (f) grams
4. (a) as heavy as   (b) heavier than
   (c) lighter than
5. S
6. (a) 100   (b) 600   (c) 250
   (d) 500   (e) 650
7. 690   8. 16
9. 370, 215   10. 540
11. 1

Word Problems

1. 385 g   2. 99 lb
3. 784 g   4. 295 g
5. 10 lb   6. 967 g
7. (a) 422 g
   (b) 926 g
8. (a) 24 oz   (b) 2 oz

Take the Challenge!

1. 1 mango equals the weight of 3 oranges. For the last picture, an orange together with a mango will have a weight that equals 4 oranges.

   From the first picture, 4 oranges only need 3 apples to balance the scale.

   Hence, in the last picture, the side with the 4 apples is heavier.

2. (a) B   (b) C

3. From the first picture, the weight of 2 □ equals the weight of 2 ♡. Hence one ♡ is needed to balance one □.

4. **Step 1:** Fill Container B with sand till it is full (3 lb). Then pour all the sand into the empty Container A. Container A would then have 3 lb of sand.

   Step 2: Fill Container B with sand again till it is full (3 lb). Then pour the sand into Container A till it is full (5 lb). What is left in Container B would be exactly 1 lb of sand.

Topic 5: Multiplication and Division

1. (a) 4   (b) 3   (c) 12
   (d) 4, 3; 4 × 3; 3; 12
2. (a) 6   (b) 2   (c) 12
   (d) 6, 2; 6 × 2; 2; 12
3. (a) 5   (b) 4   (c) 20
   (d) 5, 4; 5 × 4; 4, 4, 4, 4, 4; 20
4. (a) 3   (b) 8   (c) 24
   (d) 3, 8; 3 × 8; 8, 8, 8; 24
5. 2, 8, 16   6. 4, 10, 40
7. 3, 7, 21   8. 4, 6, 24
9. (a)
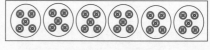
   (b)

   (c)
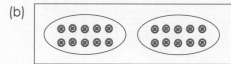
   (d)

10. (a) 6 × 4 = 24; 4 × 6 = 24
    (b) 5 × 7 = 35; 7 × 5 = 35
11. (a) 5 × 9 = 45   (b) 6 × 3 = 18
    (c) 8 × 5 = 40   (d) 10 × 3 = 30
    (e) 5 × 2 = 10   (f) 6 × 10 = 60
    (g) 4 × 3 = 12   (h) 4 × 2 = 8
    (i) 3 + 3 + 3 + 3 + 3
    (j) 9   (k) 6
    (l) 0   (m) 4 + 4 + 4
    (n) 8 + 8 + 8 + 8 + 8 + 8
    (o) 9 + 9 + 9 + 9   (p) 6
    (q) 7   (r) 5
12. 14 ÷ 2 = 7; 7   13. 12 ÷ 4 = 3; 3
14. 18 ÷ 3 = 6; 6   15. 20 ÷ 5 = 4; 4, 5
16. 30 ÷ 10 = 3; 3; 10   17. 24 ÷ 8 = 3; 3; 8
18. (a) 20 ÷ 4 = 5; 20 ÷ 5 = 4
    (b) 21 ÷ 3 = 7; 21 ÷ 7 = 3
19. 9 × 3 = 27; 3 × 9 = 27; 27 ÷ 3 = 9; 27 ÷ 9 = 3
20. (a) 12, 3, 4   (b) 16, 8, 2   (c) 5, 5, 6
    (d) 4, 4, 36   (e) 4   (f) 2

21. (a)

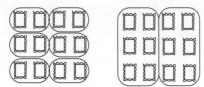

(b)

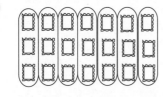

(c)

(d)

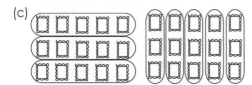

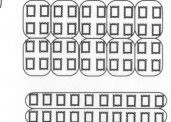

Word Problems

1. 7   2. 20   3. $27
4. 8   5. 8   6. 4

Take the Challenge!

1. 4
2. (a) 3   (b) 5
3. (a) 5   (b) 2
4. 6, 15
5. (a) 2   (b) 20

Topic 6: Multiplication Tables of 2 and 3

1. (b) 2, 2; 4
   (c) 2, 2, 2; 3 x 2; 6
   (d) 2, 2, 2, 2; 4 × 2; 8
   (e) 2, 2, 2, 2, 2; 5 × 2; 10
   (f) $6 \times 2 = 12$ (g) $7 \times 2 = 14$
   (h) $8 \times 2 = 16$ (i) $9 \times 2 = 18$
   (j) $10 \times 2 = 20$
2. (b) 2×3; 6
   (c) 3, 3, 3; 3×3; 9
   (d) 3, 3, 3, 3; 4×3; 12
   (e) 3, 3, 3, 3, 3; 5×3; 15
   (f) $6 \times 3 = 18$ (g) $7 \times 3 = 21$
   (h) $8 \times 3 = 24$ (i) $9 \times 3 = 27$
   (j) $10 \times 3 = 30$
3. (a) 6, 6   (b) 12, 12
   (c) 16, 8   (d) 15, 15
   (e) 27, 9   (f) 30, 10
4. 10, 20   5. 6, 9
6. 8   7. 10
8. 8   9. 7
10. 7
11. (a) 10, 10, 5, 2   (b) 14, 14, 7, 2
    (c) 24, 24, 8, 3   (d) 30, 3, 30, 3
12. 4, 8   13. 3
14. 8   15. 4
16. 11   17. 1, 2
18. (a) 10   (b) 7   (c) 10
    (d) 3, 15   (e) 24
19. 15, 7   20. 4
21. 9, 6   22. 21, 10
23. 2

24.

Number of boxes	1	2	5	6	9
Number of buns	2	4	10	12	18

25. 15, 8   26. $16 \div 2 = 8$
27. 8, 24   28. 11
29. 15   30. 18
31. 4, 24   32. 7, 8
33. 9   34. 7×3

35. (a)

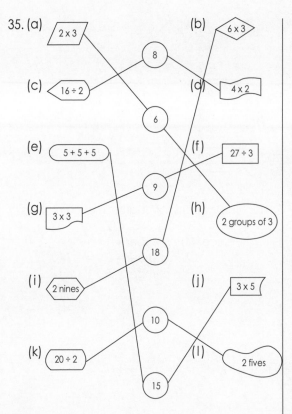

4. Circle 213, 702 5. 380
6. 17   7. 306
8. 418   9. 999
10. 139   11. 132
12. 95   13. 4
14. 4   15. C, B, A
16. 21   17. 9
18. 11   19. 14, 6

20.
Number of birds	3	9	7	5
Number of feet	6	18	14	10

21. 6   22. 8
23. 9   24. 9
25. 24, 8   26. 96
27. 30, 27   28. 4
29. R, Q, P, S
30.   3 1 5   31.   9 [8] 5
    + 5 [8] [5]   – 1 8 7
    ─────────   ─────────
       9 0 0   7 9 8

32. more than   33. equal to
34. less than
35. 940, 904, 490, 409, 49
36. B, E   37. ÷   38. –, x   39. 6   40. 3

Part 2

41. 63   42. 143
43. 4 in.   44. 240 lb
45. (a) 170 yd   (b) The park; 31 yd
46. 180 g   47. 16
48. 19 yd
49. (a) 10   (b) 5
50. (a) 21   (b) 3

More Challenging Problems

1.

	9	28	13		
	18		27		
17 10 23		10 15 25
32					19
1 13 36		8 36 6
	9		15		
	5	18	27		

2. One possible way:

2	9	4
7	5	3
6	1	8

Word Problems

1. 16
2. (a) $21
    (b) 8 days
3. 14   4. 9
5. $4   6. $16
7. 10   8. 12

Take the Challenge!

1. (a) B   (b) A   (c) C
    (d) B   (e) B   (f) C
2. [3] [9]   3. Circle 19
4. 6
5.

Mid-Year Review

Part 1

1. (a) 358
    (b) Three hundred fifty-eight
2. 40   3. Circle 87 + 245

3. (a) 2△   (b) 4△
4. (a) 89 (b) 71 (c) 21 (d) 31
    (e) 49 (f) 5 (g) 36
5. (a) ♡ = 4, ▷ = 9, ⌒ = 12

   (b) ♡ = 6, ▷ = 2, ⌒ = 10

   (c) ♡ = 7, ▷ = 13, ⌒ = 3

6. (a) 4, 3, 5 or 5, 3, 6 (b) 4, 5, 2 or 6, 3, 2
   (c) 2, 3, 4   (d) 2, 3, 6   (e) 2, 4, 5
7. 1 + 2 + 3 + 4 + 5 + 6 + 7 + 8 + 9 + 10 + 11
  + 12 = 78; 78 ÷ 2 = 39.
  The sum of the 6 numbers on each half
  must be 39.

8. ♡ = 2, ◇ = 4
9.
```
    75              72
  + 92     or     + 95
  ----            ----
   167             167
```
10.
```
    91
  - 19
  ----
    72
```
11. ♡ = 9, ☆ = 8
12. The pattern forms groups of 5 numbers:
          1, 3, 5, 4, 2
   Hence 46th number = 1
          47th number = 3
          48th number = 5